Original title:
Logs of Laughter

Copyright © 2025 Creative Arts Management OÜ
All rights reserved.

Author: Oliver Bennett
ISBN HARDBACK: 978-1-80567-270-8
ISBN PAPERBACK: 978-1-80567-569-3

The Laughter Ledger

In a world where giggles grow,
Silly jokes just steal the show.
With rubber ducks and sneaky pranks,
Joy rides in our funny banks.

Witty whispers fill the air,
Bouncing around without a care.
Whoopee cushions, rubber bands,
Fill our hearts with playful plans.

Tales of Tickles

Underneath the ticklish trees,
Jokes float softly in the breeze.
A clown with shoes too big to wear,
Makes everyone stop and stare.

Jelly beans and gummy bears,
Brings to mind our childhood cares.
Laughter echoes through the night,
Chasing shadows with delight.

Hues of Happiness

Colors dancing in the sun,
Tickling toes, oh what fun!
Rainbow slides and jolly games,
Where every giggle has no names.

Bright balloons that float on high,
Whirling past, they wave goodbye.
Every smile, a joyful spark,
Lighting up the sweetest park.

Quips and Quirks

Silly hats atop our heads,
Filling laughter in our threads.
Giggles shared with each small blunder,
Laughter rolls like distant thunder.

Nonsense poems, joyous rhymes,
Break the boredom, pass the time.
With quirks and quirks we dance about,
In this laughter, there's no doubt.

Revelry in the Rustic Realm

In a barn so bright, the cows do dance,
With moonlit smiles, they take a chance.
The pigs wear hats, a stylish crew,
While clucking hens join in, who knew?

The hay bales stack into a throne,
As raccoons play tricks, they're never alone.
The goats are singing a silly tune,
With laughter echoing, under the moon.

The Chronicles of Chuckles

A jester's cap on a squirrel's head,
He juggles acorns instead of bread.
The rabbits giggle, their tails a-fluff,
While everyone shouts, "That's just enough!"

With gopher games that never cease,
The laughter flows like a wild, sweet breeze.
Each tale spun is a twist of cheer,
In this crazy world, there's nothing to fear.

Hilarity Among the Pines

Underneath the pines, the shadows dance,
A fox tries to waltz, giving all a glance.
The owls are hooting a curious rhyme,
As crickets chirp in a comedic time.

A bear with a bowtie, quite out of place,
Trips on a branch, he quickens his pace.
With splashes of joy in every leap,
What laughter lingers before we sleep.

Giggling Shadows at Dusk

As dusk creeps in, whispers float high,
A raccoon's joke makes a rabbit cry.
With shadows stretching into the night,
The giggles echo, a pure delight.

The moon's a witness to every pun,
While owls chuckle, their work is done.
Together they weave a tapestry bright,
Of stories and laughter that fill the night.

Giggles Gathered

Bubbles bounce with every sound,
Laughter dances all around.
Tickles chase the frowns away,
In our hearts, the joy will stay.

Jokes are crafted, silly schemes,
Woven tight in golden dreams.
Friends unite in playful fights,
Crafting moments, pure delights.

Chuckle here, and giggle there,
Spreading joy into the air.
Tiny pranks and pokes abound,
With each smile, more fun is found.

Every moment wrapped in cheer,
Memories made throughout the year.
Let's remember all the jest,
And hold on tight to what is best.

The Archive of Affection

Once upon a time we laughed,
Moments shared, and joy was cast.
Tales of blunders, bloopers too,
In our hearts, they feel so true.

We recount the tricks we played,
Silly songs that never stayed.
In this vault of joyful tales,
We find humor that prevails.

Ticklish spots and goofy grins,
Stories where the fun begins.
Every giggle, every cheer,
Echoes of our fun-filled year.

As we sift through smiles and peals,
Our affection, it reveals.
Captured moments, bright and bold,
Rich with laughter to behold.

Whimsical Wonders

In a world of whimsical play,
Where chuckles chase the gloom away.
Sprinkled smiles are everywhere,
With silly hats and joyful flair.

Dancing socks and funny shoes,
Pranks disguised as little clues.
Giggling fits and playful jests,
This is where we feel our best.

Every twist leads to a grin,
In our hearts, the fun begins.
Oh, the wonders we can weave,
In our laughter, we believe.

So grab a friend and join the fun,
Underneath the shining sun.
In this realm of joy unbound,
Whimsical wonders all around.

The Diary of Delight

Each page turned, a laugh unfolds,
Stories of friendship, bold and gold.
With each doodle, joy ignites,
Moments cherished in giggly bytes.

Chronicles of silly fights,
Or secret codes and veggie bites.
A tapestry of hearty cheers,
Whisking away the weight of years.

Recalling how we danced and twirled,
In a whirl of laughter, joy unfurled.
The pages filled with pure delight,
Bringing warmth on chilly nights.

Let's pen our smiles, hearts collide,
In this diary, let's confide.
For every giggle, every tear,
Is a treasure we hold dear.

Cartwheels of Comedy

When clowns collide in silly games,
Their pratfalls echo, no one's to blame.
Juggling pies high under the moon,
Laughter erupts, a joyous tune.

Bananas slip with every cheer,
As giggles soar, they have no fear.
With sprinkles flying, bright and bold,
Their happiness is pure gold.

A ticklish breeze whispers delight,
While funny hats take off in flight.
Acrobats bend, faces with glee,
A circus of smiles, wild and free.

In this realm of vast surprise,
Every joke wears a goofy guise.
The fun we find, a treasure chest,
In the antics, we are truly blessed.

Testament of Tickles

Underneath the bright big top,
A little monkey takes a hop.
With tiny feet and playful glee,
He dances wildly, oh, so free.

A tickle monster prowls the ground,
While giggles echo all around.
Fuzzy socks and silly shoes,
In every laugh, we just can't lose.

Wobbling sheep jump on a stage,
Their laughter spreads, a joyful rage.
Pie in the face, it's not a crime,
For every chuckle brings the rhyme.

Each twist and turn sparks delight,
In the world of fun, we take flight.
A testament made of joy and play,
With every smile, we seize the day.

The Mosaic of Mirth

A tapestry woven with cheerful cheers,
With every giggle, erasing fears.
Colorful jests like paint on a wall,
Creating smiles, inviting all.

Twirling around in vibrant hues,
A jester sings with silly views.
Juggling dreams, the crowd takes a chance,
In this quirky, festive dance.

Each moment stitched with hearty laughs,
We find joy in our goofy drafts.
With marzipan hats and flowery shoes,
In this mosaic, we cannot lose.

So let's embrace this vibrant play,
Where the silly breeze carries us away.
Through patchwork joy, we'll ever roam,
In laughter's land, we find our home.

Serenade of Snickers

In the park, a puppy prances,
With floppy ears, he takes his chances.
Chasing tails and butterflies,
In every bark, pure joy flies.

A family picnic, blankets spread wide,
With jelly sandwiches, smiles can't hide.
As ants march by, a comic scene,
Sprinkling fun, a joy machine.

Silly faces, we pull and stretch,
In a game of charades, we all are fetched.
Tickled by thoughts, we can't resist,
In this serenade, we coexist.

With every snicker, a connection made,
Creating memories, never to fade.
Together we laugh until it stings,
In the cadence of joy, our spirit sings.

Rhapsody of Raucous Joy

In a circus of chuckles, we play,
With clowns that tumble, oh what a day!
Juggling jokes that bounce and soar,
Laughter erupts, wanting more.

A parrot squawks with a comical flair,
Telling tall tales that fill the air.
Tripping on puns, we tumble and roll,
Jovial spirits that lighten the soul.

Snapshots of glee dance in our heads,
Each giggle and snort, a joy that spreads.
Tickled pink by the whispers of cheer,
A rhapsody blossoming, oh so clear!

When laughter's the music, we dance along,
With rhymes that bubble like a merry song.
In this carnival of fun, we unite,
Creating memories that feel so bright.

The Archive of Amusement

In a dusty nook, where the humor lies,
Stories of chuckles take to the skies.
A library filled with giggles and cheer,
Catalogued moments we hold so dear.

A rubber chicken greets you with glee,
Tickling memories, wild and free.
Bonkers antics in pages unfold,
Hilarious tales forever retold.

Flip through the album of silly spritz,
Where laughter is captured, no need for scripts.
Silly hats and wacky pranks shine,
In this archive, hilarity's divine!

Each snapshot a treasure, a funny refrain,
With echoes of laughter that dance in the rain.
So dive in the humor, let your spirit swim,
In the archive of joy, where the lights never dim.

Hilarity's Haven

In a castle of giggles, we roam about,
With walls that whisper, "No room for doubt."
Jesters laughing, their tricks all around,
This haven of humor, where joy can be found.

A slide made of snickers, a swing of delight,
We revel in moments that feel just right.
Chasing our shadows, we burst into song,
In hilarity's haven, we all belong.

Ticklish treasures under every chair,
With zany inventions floating in air.
Crafting our laughter in bright, silly hues,
Where joy is the language, the heart's only muse.

So come take a seat, pull a joke from the shelf,
In this tapestry woven of laughter itself.
With every new twist, we giggle and cheer,
In hilarity's haven, there's nothing to fear!

Whirlwind of Wit

In a swirl of snickers, the fun begins,
Words take flight like mischievous twins.
Puns like confetti, they dance and twirl,
A whirlwind of wit around us unfurl.

Silly surprises in every nook,
With punchlines popping like a fine-cooked book.
Barrels of laughter, let's fill to the brim,
In this tornado of joy, we merrily swim.

Chasing the storm of quirky delight,
With quips and comebacks that soar to new height.
Fairy tales twist into ludicrous views,
A whirlwind of fun that we all can peruse.

So join us, dear friend, let the laughter flow,
In this wacky abyss where the good times grow.
With every jest crafted, we'll never grow dim,
In the whirlwind of wit, let the joy begin!

Eloquent Echoes of Euphoria

In shadows where giggles creep,
Funny tales begin to leap.
Tickles shared in hushed delight,
Laughter dances through the night.

Gaffes and glimmers, bright and bold,
Stories spun of magic told.
Friends around, the jesters play,
Echoes bounce in merry dismay.

A wink, a nod, a playful jest,
Humor finds the very best.
Disarray and whimsy's charms,
Laughter's grip, the world disarms.

In the garden of pure cheer,
Joyful moments gather near.
With every chuckle, life's a dream,
In the silliness, we beam.

Jester's Journal

A cap and bells, a tongue so quick,
In every line, a witty trick.
The jester prances, leaps around,
In laughter's arms, we all are bound.

With pratfalls carved in silly prose,
Every blunder, laughter grows.
Tales of whoops and howlers bright,
In jest we find our hearts take flight.

Oh, the joy a smile can bring,
In every word, a foolish fling.
Dance of puns and playful ways,
Life's a stage where humor plays.

With friends who giggle, snorts and winks,
We weave the fabric of our links.
In this journal, we declare,
A funny world beyond compare.

Radiance in Reverie

Bright thoughts like bubbles, float and glide,
In gentle waves of joy, we ride.
Reflecting light, a radiant grin,
Moments captured, laughter's kin.

The past brings forth a silly glance,
With every twist, the giggles dance.
Dreams entwined with bright mirth's glow,
In the realm where chuckles flow.

Witty banter, ripples spread,
A symphony of joys ahead.
In reverie's embrace we twirl,
Life's vibrant hues, a merry swirl.

As starlit nights cast shadows down,
We crown our days with humor's crown.
Radiance shines where laughter's found,
In joyous echoes, hearts abound.

Cairn of Cheer

Stacked high, the stones of laughter rest,
Each one a tale, a cherished jest.
On this mound of joy we stand,
Building memories, hand in hand.

With every chuckle, the cairn grows wide,
A fortress built where fun won't hide.
Foundations laid in comic glee,
Together, we shape our history.

When life gets tough and skies turn gray,
We gather 'round, fun leads the way.
With humor's charm, we mend and cheer,
In this castle, we hold dear.

Atop this pile of playful stone,
We celebrate the laughter grown.
A tapestry woven with joy and grace,
In our haven, we find our place.

The Archive of Amusement

In the shelf of jesters' tunes,
Laughter hides with crazy spoons.
Whispers echo, jokes unwind,
Tickles dance, and giggles find.

Silly hats and wobbly shoes,
Curly mustaches, mixed up views.
Every page, a haphazard cheer,
In this vault, the fun appears.

Pranks that leap from every crack,
Banana peels on the track.
The laughter spins in full delight,
Chasing shadows, chasing light.

Step inside and you shall see,
Where every chuckle plays with glee.
In this archive, happiness reigns,
A world where humor never wanes.

Fables of Frolic

Once a duck with shoes too tight,
Tripped and stumbled through the night.
With each fall, a cheeky quack,
The moonlight laughed, it had no lack.

A cat that dreamed of being tall,
Climbed a tree then took a fall.
Sailed the breeze, a purring cheer,
All the squirrels stopped to peer.

A frog in shades, quite out of place,
Hopped along with style and grace.
Croaked a tune of pure delight,
Making stars giggle with the night.

These fables told in playful song,
Where silliness just can't be wrong.
Join the dance of whimsy's might,
In these tales of sheer delight.

Tidal Waves of Tittering

A wave of chuckles rolls ashore,
Lifting spirits, wanting more.
Each splash a grin, a gleeful shout,
Waves of joy we can't live without.

Sailing boats made of pure laughter,
Navigating the sea, a humorous chapter.
Seagulls sing with a cheeky flair,
Ticklish breezes fill the air.

Ducklings paddling in a line,
Slipping on a joke so fine.
Every ripple, a story spun,
In the tide, the fun has begun.

Join the surf, take the plunge,
Where giggles crash and fears expunge.
In this ocean, carefree and free,
Ride the waves of jubilee.

Mirthful Memories

Snapshots of joy, a playful scene,
Captured smiles, silly and keen.
Laughter bubbles in every frame,
Stories shared, never the same.

Birthday cakes that flew on high,
Squeaky voices trying to fly.
Confetti storms and piñata bliss,
In this gallery, none can miss.

A dog with glasses on its face,
Chasing squirrels at a frantic pace.
The goofy dance of Grandma's feet,
Every memory, bittersweet.

So gather round, let's reminisce,
In every laugh, a little bliss.
Mirthful times we hold so dear,
In the heart, they always cheer.

The Carnival of Chuckling

Balloons ascend with goofy grins,
A clown trips over his floppy shoes.
Laughter erupts from all around,
In this joyful game, we cannot lose.

Cotton candy clouds float in the air,
Silly hats atop our heads just right.
Each giggle mirrors the vibrant hues,
As we dance in the glow of twilight.

Twists and turns on the funhouse ride,
Strange mirrors reflect our silly side.
We tumble and fall, but never mind,
In this merry land, we all abide.

The jester juggles with vibrant flair,
Pranks and puns fill the cheerful scene.
A raucous chorus of laughter shared,
Creating memories, light and keen.

Resonance of Raucousness

Echoes bounce off the circus walls,
As laughter bursts like popping corn.
Humor pirouettes, joyous and free,
In every smile, a new joy is born.

The pie in the face, what a sight to see,
Giggling friends on the ground do lay.
Prancing dogs in silly hats,
Chasing tails in their playful sway.

A magical act with slips and trips,
The grand maestro spins round and round.
We can't help but laugh from our very souls,
In this realm where silliness is found.

Frogs on bicycles, what a delight,
Their little legs paddling fast and bright.
As the band strikes up a goofy tune,
Together we dance under the moon.

Whispers of Playful Echoes

Tiny giggles ripple through the air,
Twinkling eyes ignite the playful night.
Joyful whispers weave their threads of fun,
In this laughter, everything feels right.

Silly string flies in all directions,
A cascade of color, a vibrant mess.
Side-splitting stories shared with glee,
Time stands still in this moment, no less.

A parade of antics marches on,
With each prank, a memory to make.
We chase the shadows, we hide, we seek,
In this joyful world, all laughter awake.

Banana peels on the pavement wait,
With every slip, more laughter is born.
Tickled hearts embrace the silly times,
In echoes of play, we're forever sworn.

Jests Beneath the Canopy

Under the tent where the funny men flow,
A joke told here sets the crowd aglow.
Frolicsome jesters dance in delight,
As we giggle into the beautiful night.

Echoes of laughter bounce from the trees,
Swaying branches join the infectious tease.
A puppet show springs to life, so grand,
With each tiny gesture, we all understand.

The tug on a string leads us to cheer,
Unexpected gags that bring all the jeers.
Everyone's face is lit with delight,
Wrapped in the warmth of a shared funny sight.

Tickling tales carried on the breeze,
Sparkling eyes like stars in the dark seas.
As night falls softly, the laughter remains,
Under the canopy, joy still reigns.

The Forest's Joyful Murmurs

In the shade where whispers play,
Squirrels jest and leap all day.
With acorns tossed and friendly shouts,
Nature's humor never doubts.

The brook giggles, skips along,
A melody of nature's song.
Birds chirp jokes in feathered flight,
Making every heart feel light.

Beneath the trees, a dance ensues,
Wind and leaves join in the ruse.
The earth chuckles, bright and gay,
In this lively, leafy sway.

Mushrooms giggle, mushrooms grin,
As playful shadows dance within.
Each corner holds a silly sight,
In the woods, all hearts take flight.

Tales of Merriment in the Wilderness

Frogs in ponds with croaks of cheer,
Telling stories to all who hear.
A rabbit winks, a fox wears a grin,
In this realm, laughter's the greatest win.

The sun peeks through with a playful beam,
Casting shadows that dance and gleam.
Each rustle, a secret tickled by air,
Sending giggles soaring everywhere.

Old oak trees share jokes from the past,
Their bark cracking with each hearty laugh.
Butterflies flutter, teasing with glee,
As mischief blooms beneath each tree.

Every step taken, a chuckle unfolds,
In nature's grasp, joy never grows old.
And as night falls, stars begin to wink,
Leaving tales that make your heart think.

Echoes of Enchantment and Delight

Moonbeams dance on the forest floor,
Filling the night with a giggling roar.
Crickets chirp in quirky tones,
While laughter frolics among the stones.

The path ahead is lined with cheer,
Each twig snaps with a joke to hear.
From shadows long the sprites emerge,
In a playful dance, they intertwine and surge.

Whimsical whispers ripple the breeze,
Tickling the branches on the trees.
Every rustle hides a merry sound,
Where joy and whimsy can be found.

Fireflies flicker with stories untold,
Creating magic, pure and bold.
In this enchanting, mirthful night,
Every heart feels the pure delight.

Chuckling Leaves in the Breeze

Leaves laugh lightly as they spin,
Whispering secrets, inviting you in.
A dance of nature, swift and free,
Where giggles chase each tiny bee.

The sunbeams scatter like scattered seeds,
Filling the air with whimsical deeds.
Flowers beam with a colorful grin,
As petals flutter, let the fun begin!

Breezy winds carry chuckles far,
Echoing softly around each star.
Nature unfolds a humorous tale,
Where even the quiet trees unveil.

With every step, joy's scent is near,
In this bright woodland, laughter's clear.
So follow the sounds of fun that tease,
Hear the chuckles of leaves in the breeze.

Silliness Between the Trees

In a forest where jokes play,
Trees whisper secrets of the day.
Squirrels dance with acorn hats,
While the owls chuckle, „What's up with that?"

Beneath the boughs, shadows tango,
Marshmallow clouds in a funny jangle.
Bunnies hop with comical ease,
Telling tales that tickle the breeze.

The sun breaks through in a golden glow,
Laughter bubbles, and worries go.
At twilight, the fireflies start to tease,
Blowing kisses from the giggling trees.

The Giggle Grove Diaries

Once there lived a cheeky crow,
Who stole hats from folks below.
Witty bears played hide and seek,
With bursts of laughter, oh so unique.

A porcupine in a tutu pranced,
While rabbits in sunhats mischievously danced.
The brook babbled jokes with a splash,
As nature giggled; life was a bash.

At dusk, the critters held a show,
With silly acts and humorous flow.
In every nook, a joy to find,
Jubilant echoes, forever entwined.

Mirth Under the Moonlit Boughs

Moonlight spilled on the twinkling leaves,
Casting shadows that giggle and tease.
Woodland friends in costumes so bright,
Juggling fireflies, oh what a sight!

A clumsy fox trips, laughter erupts,
As wise old turtles share jokes, interrupt.
The breeze hums tunes that spin in delight,
While the crickets play chords in the night.

Stars wink down in a playful manner,
Wishing upon jokes that still make us stammer.
With hearts full of joy, we dance and we sway,
In the mirthful woods where we laugh the night away.

Frolics in the Wooded Nook

In a cozy nook where giggles thrive,
Chirping birds cheerfully arrive.
Badgers spin grand tales of woe,
While beetles play tag, dodging to and fro.

A playful breeze tickles our ears,
Unraveling whispers, laughter and cheers.
The sunbeams play hide-and-seek,
Turning the ordinary into a sneak peak.

With swings made of vines, we soar up high,
As butterflies twirl and clouds drift by.
In this wooded haven so carefree and bright,
We create our own joy, wrapped in pure light.

Mirthful Musings

In a world where giggles bloom,
And joy chases away all gloom,
A jester's hat twirls in the night,
As laughter dances, pure delight.

With puns that tickle and tease,
We gather 'neath the laughter trees,
Each chuckle builds a silly tower,
In this comic, magical hour.

A cat in socks slips on the floor,
While rubber ducks begin to soar,
Silly hats and quippy tones,
Funny bones and joyful groans.

In the end, we gather round,
Belly laughs are all we found,
Sharing stories, light as air,
In mirthful moments, none compare.

The Codex of Chuckles

Open the book of giggles bright,
Where silly tales take silly flight,
A monkey slips on a banana peel,
And every laugh becomes a reel.

Whimsical scribbles, clownish art,
Each note a chuckle, warm to the heart,
With rubber chickens, pie-filled frays,
Comic capers unfold in waves.

Each page a dance of giddy cheer,
With knock-knock jokes that draw us near,
In this codex of joyful cheer,
Find the laughter we hold dear.

So gather 'round, chuckle and snort,
In this merry, jolly court,
Where every line brings a smile,
Let's share the joy, stay a while.

Tales of Tickle-induced Trance

In the land where giggles reign,
Each ticklish tale breaks every chain,
A frog sings opera, quite absurd,
While silly squirrels dance, unheard.

The sun wears shades, a sight to see,
While turtles race, pretending free,
With hat tricks and pratfalls, such finesse,
In this trance of humor, nothing less.

Stories spin like tops in the breeze,
With winks and jests that aim to please,
A waterfall of fits and glee,
In every corner, laughter's key.

So join this laughable parade,
With jesters on the grand charade,
In tales where happiness takes chance,
And we surrender to the trance.

The Symphony of Smiles

In the orchestra of glee, we play,
Each laugh a note, come what may,
A symphony of joy unfolds,
As funny moments take their hold.

With tickles strumming on a lyre,
And jokes that soar, never tire,
A blend of giggles, snorts, and grins,
In harmony, together wins.

The cymbals clash with every pun,
As laughter rings, we have our fun,
And in this grand, melodic spree,
Every chuckle sets us free.

So gather close, let laughter swell,
In this symphony, all is well,
With smiles that echo 'round the bends,
In joyous rhythms, laughter blends.

The Chronicles of Chuckles

In a land where giggles reign,
Tickles dance like crazy trains.
Jokes travel far, from ear to ear,
Laughter echoes, spreading cheer.

Silly hats and pratfalls too,
Every moment shines anew.
With each twist, a smile appears,
Joy erupts, dismissing fears.

Banters fly like butterflies,
Wit ignites the bluest skies.
Amidst the games and playful pranks,
We gather joy in merry ranks.

The stories told, both bold and bright,
Turn mundane days to sheer delight.
So let us share this wild spree,
Where laughter builds community.

Canvas of Cheerfulness

Brushstrokes of joy, a vibrant sway,
Colors burst in a grand display.
Giggles spill like paint from tubes,
Creating scenes of happy moods.

Each canvas tells of a funny tale,
Where blunders and jests easily sail.
Splatters and smudges, mistakes divine,
Turned into treasures, oh how they shine!

Chasing rainbows, chasing dreams,
Witty quips and silly schemes.
In every corner, a chuckle waits,
Life's a party at art's gates.

Grins like hues, bright and bold,
In every stroke, a joy retold.
So gather 'round, the canvas calls,
With laughter echoing in the halls.

Stacks of Smiles

Piled high on a shelf of cheer,
Each grin a treasure, vivid and dear.
From silly tales of cats in hats,
To joke-filled boxes where laughter bats.

One smile stacked, then two, then three,
Crafting joy like a booming spree.
As friends unpack these joyous wiles,
Filling rooms with stacks of smiles.

Every chuckle, a brick in the wall,
Building up dreams, standing tall.
We forge a fortress, fun-filled light,
With laughter echoing into the night.

So add a grin, don't let it cease,
In every corner, find your peace.
Together we rise, as stories unite,
Transforming moments into pure delight.

Reflections of Revelry

Mirrors gleam with joyous sights,
Reflecting back our silly flights.
In playful jest, we twist and shout,
Laughter ripples, without a doubt.

Each giggle waves like water's gleam,
Creating quite a merry dream.
In moments shared, we find our spark,
Turning the mundane into the lark.

Revelry whispers through the air,
Cackles dance like a carefree flair.
In every glance, our spirits bloom,
Filling hearts and every room.

So take a leap, embrace the fun,
With laughter's glow, our hearts are won.
In this reflection, we are found,
Joy resonates, profoundly bound.

The Dial of Delight

A tickle here, a giggle there,
A twist of fate with moments rare.
The clock spins round, a merry race,
We find ourselves in laughter's embrace.

Bubbles burst, and jokes take flight,
Brightening up the dullest night.
With every chime, our giggles grow,
A symphony of joy in tow.

Silly faces, playful pranks,
We dance around, giving thanks.
For every chuckle, every cheer,
We spin the wheel of joy, my dear.

A wink, a nod, a laugh so bold,
In this parade, let stories unfold.
In every heart, a spark ignites,
A melody of fun that delights.

Rhythms of Revelry

In a world where laughter reigns,
We find the joy in silly gains.
Tickles and pranks fill up the air,
An orchestra of happiness, we share.

Rhythms dance, a playful tune,
We sway beneath the laughter's moon.
Each chuckle writes a verse anew,
In every heart, a spirit grew.

Loud belly laughs and snorts of glee,
Unruly joy, wild and free.
With every beat, let worries fade,
As we celebrate this fun parade.

Chasing dreams on feet so light,
A cascading wave of pure delight.
For every smile, a story we'll tell,
In this playful world, we cast our spell.

Piles of Playful Spirit

A mountain high of jokes to share,
In laughter's land, we're without care.
With every jest, our spirits soar,
We tumble forth, seeking more.

Silly hats and bright balloons,
We dance beneath the laughing moons.
Catching giggles like fireflies,
In this realm, no tearful sighs.

Each punchline lands with gentle grace,
A joyful game we gladly chase.
In playful piles, our giggles blend,
In this funny world, there's no end.

From whispers soft to roaring glee,
We weave our tapestry, wild and free.
In every heart, laughter can spark,
Creating joy that leaves a mark.

Silhouettes of Smiles

In sunset hues, the smiles take flight,
Casting shadows in golden light.
With every grin, a tale unfolds,
A comic strip of joys retold.

Echoes of laughter twirl and sway,
We paint the skies in a playful way.
Every chuckle, a brushstroke fine,
Creating art where spirits shine.

Jests exchanged in playful haste,
Sweet moments lived, none to waste.
In silhouettes of pure delight,
We dance along, hearts feeling light.

With mischief made, we take our chance,
In a world where joy makes us dance.
Together we'll weave, create, and smile,
In this vibrant life, we'll go that extra mile.

The Joyful Journey

In a car that won't stop bouncing,
We laugh as snacks go flying,
A dog joins in our prancing,
While the GPS keeps lying.

With a map that's all but wrinkled,
And songs so off-key we sing,
Every bump and turn we crinkled,
Turns the ride to a wild fling.

Yet we chase those silly moments,
As the road winds ever long,
Each giggle builds an endowment,
In a life that's a comical song.

So through fields and hills we're going,
With smiles stretched from ear to ear,
In this laughter-filled showing,
Every stop brings more good cheer.

Moments of Merriment

A pie that flies through the kitchen,
With a grin and a quick little toss,
It lands, oh dear, how bewitching,
On the dog's head, what a loss!

A juggler tries with a flair,
But the fruit does not quite comply,
Bananas and apples in air,
It's a sight that makes us all cry.

At the picnic, ants steal the scene,
They march in lines, quite the parade,
We laugh till our faces turn green,
As our sandwiches swiftly degrade.

This dance of mishaps brings glee,
In a world where the silly thrives,
Each moment holds a key,
To the joy that forever survives.

The Bulletin of Banter

Gather 'round for the gossip,
About the cat who steals the show,
With a leap and a graceful flop,
She claims her throne and won't let go.

Our neighbor's lawn looks like a jungle,
With flamingos lined up in rows,
We can't help but break into a chuckle,
At the gardener's strange little woes.

The mailman trips, his bag goes soaring,
Letters rain down all around,
He laughs as he keeps on ignoring,
The puppy's chase on the ground.

Each tale we share adds to the fun,
A tapestry of playful jest,
With laughter that's never quite done,
These moments become our very best.

Anecdotes of Amusements

Once there was a frog in a hat,
Who dreamed of being quite a star,
With leaps and bounds, oh, how he sat,
In the spotlight of a makeshift bar.

A penguin wobbled through the door,
With a drink made of fish, oh so bright,
He raised his flipper, wanting more,
While the crowd laughed at this sight.

A turtle tried to dance with flair,
But tripped and rolled on the ground,
Each tumble met with playful air,
As we cheered for his silly surround.

These stories weave joy together,
In a quilt of chuckles and glee,
Through each funny unexpected tether,
We find love in our jubilee.

Hilarious Hues of Nature's Palette

In fields where daisies dance with glee,
A bumblebee wears a coat of spree.
The sun tickles clouds, they giggle and twirl,
As daisies chuckle, in soft petals unfurl.

A squirrel with acorns, a jester so spry,
Flips in the air, oh my, how they fly!
The rainbow stretches, a bow of delight,
Colors sing loud under nature's spotlight.

On mossy rocks, the frogs croak in jest,
With each silly leap, they give it their best.
The wind carries laughter, like notes from a flute,
Nature relishes joy, so sweet and so cute.

Beneath the bright blossoms, the giggles cascade,
Each bloom with a secret, a joke well portrayed.
From morning till dusk, the humor takes hold,
In nature's grand canvas, a story unfolds.

The Warmth of Whispered Whimsy

The sun peeks through trees, with a grin on its face,
    Casting warm shadows, a radiant embrace.
    A rabbit hops by, wearing socks on its feet,
    While butterflies giggle, a whimsical treat.

    Under the branches, the squirrels conspire,
        Spinning their tales around a campfire.
    The wind joins in, with a tickle and tease,
    Turning each moment into pure, silly ease.

    A snail in a top hat, with a swagger so bold,
        Winks at a ladybug, its humor retold.
    The laughter of nature, a melody bright,
    Whispers of whimsy, like stars in the night.

In the heart of the grove, where the children all play,
    They chase after shadows, both silly and fey.
    With giggling echoes that bubble and flow,
The warmth of these whispers makes spirits aglow.

Glee Beneath the Arboreal Canopy

In the shade of the trees, where shadows unfold,
Laughter erupts, a treasure untold.
The owls swap tales with a chuckle and wink,
While chipmunks gather, their cheeks full of pink.

The brook bubbling brightly joins in the fun,
Bouncing along, under rays of the sun.
Each splash like a giggle, each ripple a cheer,
In this woodland theatre, there's joy everywhere.

The ants hold a dance beneath roots so wide,
With twirls and with leaps, they take fate in stride.
The leaves rustle softly, a chorus divine,
Singing sweet songs of their quirky design.

Beneath the green canopy, laughter takes flight,
As critters unite, in this magical night.
With smiles all around, they gather and play,
Glee reigns supreme, come what may!

The Playful Spirit of the Glade

In a glade full of laughter and whimsical cheer,
The rabbits play charades, snickering near.
The flowers all giggle, with colors so bright,
In this playful arena, they dance in delight.

A frog in a crown strikes a royal pose,
While crickets provide the music that grows.
The trees sway to rhythms, their branches a sway,
Inviting the critters to join in the play.

A hedgehog with spectacles reads from a book,
With tales of adventure, come take a look!
The fireflies sparkle, their glow full of grace,
Filling the night with a dance to embrace.

As moonlight pours down on this joyous expanse,
Creatures unite for a playful romance.
In the spirit of fun, every heart finds a friend,
In this glade of delight, where smiles never end.

Laughing Prints on the Earth

In the meadow, giggles sprout,
Tiny critters dance about.
Bouncing bugs with silly glee,
Nature's jesters, wild and free.

Shadows play in the warm sun,
Every leaf laughs, joins the fun.
Rippling streams with chuckles bright,
Greet the day with pure delight.

A squirrel jokes, a bird does sing,
Every creature's a clown, it seems.
The grass whispers playful hints,
In this world, nothing repents.

With every step, laughter blooms,
Tickling the earth's quiet rooms.
Come take a walk, leave worries bare,
In nature's laughter, find your care.

Cheerful Whispers of the Wild

In the trees, the wind does tease,
A rustle here, a rustle please.
The foxes grin, the owls chuckle,
Every nook holds a happy buckle.

Merry birds on branches swing,
Singing songs that make hearts sing.
The butterflies twirl, a lovely sight,
Painting the air with colors bright.

Roots tap dance beneath the ground,
Swaying softly, making sound.
The brook babbles with a joke,
In nature's realm, the laughter's woke.

Clouds drift by, with fluffy cheer,
Whispering secrets that all can hear.
Wherever you roam, smiles you'll find,
In this wild, happiness is kind.

The Jolly Journey of Nature's Footsteps

With every step, the earth does grin,
Footprints left where joy begins.
The daisies nod in bright array,
In this journey, let's laugh and play.

The hills roll with a jovial sway,
As the sun peeks through the day.
Breezes giggle, tickling our hair,
Taking us along without a care.

Winding paths lead to shared delight,
Every turn, a surprise in sight.
Barks of trees in friendly tone,
Remind us we're never alone.

March along, beneath skies so blue,
Nature's humor is a gift for you.
Join the dance, be wild, be free,
With laughter echoing endlessly.

Forest Frivolities and Folly

In the heart of the laughing grove,
Silly tales and secrets rove.
Missteps of deer bring giggles loud,
Nature's court is a joyful crowd.

Frogs wear crowns, and owls are wise,
Dancing shadows under clear skies.
The mushrooms jest, their caps held high,
In this land where spirits fly.

Leaves fall like tickles, soft and sweet,
Squirrels scramble on tiny feet.
Each rustle and rattle a comic scene,
In this frolicsome, wild machine.

So step with cheer on this vibrant floor,
Where laughter flows and troubles bore.
Behold the whimsy all around,
In folly found, joy is profound.

Recollections of Radiance

In the park, a squirrel danced,
Chasing shadows, it pranced.
With acorns flying through the air,
A circus act beyond compare.

The dog next door wore a hat,
Chasing its tail, a silly spat.
Neighbors gathered, all in glee,
To witness such absurdity.

A cat on a board, surfing waves,
The whole street burst out, so brave.
With laughter ringing through the night,
Our worries vanished, all felt right.

Each silly tale, a spark so bright,
Filling hearts with pure delight.
From silly faces to tiny quirks,
In these moments, laughter lurks.

Laughter's Lantern

A penguin slipped on ice so slick,
Landing in snow, what a trick!
Everyone burst into applause,
For the humor that nature draws.

The chicken crossed, but with a twist,
On roller skates, it couldn't resist.
Fowls wobbling left and right,
A show that lit up the night.

A grandma danced with jelly beans,
Her wiggly hips were fit for queens.
With each step, the world would grin,
As she spun round with a joyful spin.

A dog that barked, a cat that sang,
Under the stars, pure joy rang.
With every chuckle, a story spun,
Reminding us life's all in fun.

The Joyous Journal

Each morning brings a goofy sight,
A goat in boots, what a delight!
It trotted proud, a sight to see,
Our giggles echoed with such glee.

The bicycle once met a duck,
They pedaled hard, oh what luck!
The quacking matched the wheel's loud spin,
A tale of friendship that made us grin.

A mishap with a banana peel,
Left grandpa wobbly, what a deal!
With laughter streaming from his chest,
He took a bow, he was the best.

At sunset's glow, we shared our chats,
Of silly times, and playful spats.
These moments penned in fun and cheer,
Will forever warm the heart, my dear.

Mirthful Melodies

The piano played, but out it jumped,
A bunny bounced, and all were stumped.
With every hop, it played a note,
We laughed till tears began to float.

A cat with shades, so cool and bright,
Strutting confidently through the night.
With swagger that was off the chart,
It stole our laughter, touched our heart.

A fish in a bowl tried to dance,
Swirling water, what a chance!
Splashes flying, giggles in the air,
A fishy rhythm beyond compare.

Each twinkle, each breeze, a joyful tune,
Guided by laughter beneath the moon.
With every rhyme and silly jest,
We find our spirits truly blessed.

Chronicles of Bliss

In the middle of a bustling town,
A jester danced with a floppy crown.
His shoes were huge, a clownish sight,
Laughter echoed into the night.

A cat in a hat, a squirrel with flair,
Chasing each other without a care.
They flipped and flopped, a silly race,
Smiles sprouted on every face.

A baby laughed at a tickling breeze,
While a dog chased shadows among the trees.
Every corner was filled with glee,
Bubbles floated, wild and free.

Even the moon quirked a grin,
As the stars blushed at the cheerful din.
These moments we hold, a treasure chest,
In the chronicles, we laugh the best.

The Cove of Chuckles

Down by the shore where the tides rise,
A crab put on glasses to everyone's surprise.
He strutted around like he owned the sand,
Making folks giggle with a wave of his hand.

A parrot recited poems so absurd,
He'd caw and he'd cackle, each line a word.
Nearby, a dog, with a soggy sock,
Was prancing about, a quirky rock.

The wind told jokes between the trees,
It rustled the leaves with teasing ease.
Kids made castles from laughter and foam,
Each ripple of joy, a makeshift home.

As the sun dipped low, shadows did dance,
Drawing out chuckles in a merry prance.
In this cove, the heart stays light,
With echoes of giggles, pure delight.

The Reservoir of Rapture

In a park where the daisies sway and bloom,
Lives a squirrel with a penchant for zoom.
He bounces about, his cheeks stuffed wide,
With nuts piled high, he cannot hide.

A boy with a kite flew high in the air,
But it tangled in trees and gave quite a scare.
With a twist and a turn, laughter did burst,
As the kite floated down, a comical first.

Joggers tripped over feet in a race,
Each tumble a story, brightening the space.
The sun beamed warmly, encouraging fun,
As echoes of joy danced, one by one.

This reservoir flows with giggles and cheers,
Washing away grief, calming all fears.
In each hearty chuckle, we find our way,
Seeding tomorrow with bright rays of play.

Rendezvous with Joy

A party of frogs on a lily pad throne,
Croaked funny tunes in a ribbiting tone.
They jumped in a line, a whimsical show,
Each leap brought forth a laugh and a glow.

Nearby, a mouse caught a whiff of a pie,
He plotted and schemed, oh my, oh my!
With a dash and a dive, he snagged a slice,
And turned every morsel into a heist!

A patchwork of friends from different lands,
Shared tales of the goofiest, luckiest plans.
With every recount, the laughter grew wide,
A carnival of chuckles, hearts open wide.

As night cloaked the heavens in twinkling light,
Joy danced around, a beautiful sight.
In this rendezvous, we find our true spark,
As laughter ignites the once quiet dark.

Laughter's Landscape

In fields of giggles, joy does sprout,
Where silly whispers dance about.
A jester's cap flaps in the breeze,
While chuckles tumble from the trees.

Like buttered bread on a sunny plate,
Each snicker spreads in perfect fate.
With tickled toes and grinning eyes,
We chase the clouds in playful skies.

Backyard tales of wonder roam,
In a sandbox, each laugh feels like home.
A painted top hat, bright and bold,
Hides treasures of humor yet untold.

So join the merry, don't be shy,
Let your laughter lift and fly.
In this landscape where joy prevails,
The heart sings sweet in ticklish trails.

Gala of Glee

Amidst the twirls of vibrant cheer,
Guests gather 'round, all full of beer.
With quirky ties and silly hats,
The air is thick with joyous chats.

A dance-off breaks, all out of sync,
With every move, the laughter's pink.
A pie in the face, oh what a sight,
Each playful jab brings pure delight.

The punchline lands, and giggles swell,
As friends trade stories, oh so well.
A jester juggles, the crowd does lean,
For in this gala, life is keen.

So raise a glass to fun-filled nights,
Where laughter beams and spirit ignites.
A joyous occasion, bright and free,
In this gala, we simply must be.

The Cornucopia of Comicality

A feast of jokes laid on the table,
With puns and gags, we're more than able.
Each slice of humor, a hearty bite,
Served with a wink, oh what delight!

A turkey trips, and laughter bursts,
While mashed potatoes bubble and rust.
Green beans dance in acrobatic style,
At this banquet, we grin all the while.

The punchbowl brims with stories spun,
Each tale more silly than the one.
In this cornucopia, joy runs wild,
And every guest feels like a child.

So gather 'round, let the fun begin,
With laughter and cheer, we surely win.
In a harvest of giggles, hearts so light,
We relish the whimsy found tonight.

Yarns of Yielded Yuks

With every thread, a tale unfolds,
A tapestry bright with laughs untold.
Old socks and stories, a comical blend,
Where punchlines twist and never end.

A grandparent's tale of youthful spree,
Leaves us all in fits of glee.
Next, a cat with a hat so grand,
Strutting about, it takes a stand.

Every chuckle, a stitch we weave,
In this fabric of joy, we believe.
With humor's yarn, we craft our day,
In each little laugh, we find our way.

So grab a seat, and lend an ear,
As stories tumble, never fear.
Through yuks and giggles, we stitch anew,
In this cozy quilt, there's room for you.

Jubilant Echoes

In the field where laughter blooms,
A chicken dances, then resumes.
With wobbly legs it shakes a wing,
As silly songs the voices sing.

A goat in pajamas hops and prances,
While everyone around him glances.
Tickled ribs and gasping breaths,
The giggles slow to whispered depths.

A jester's hat at a neighbor's door,
A pie in the face, oh what a score!
With every chuckle, every cheer,
Laughter spreads, it's what we hear.

So join the fun, let spirits soar,
For in this world, who could ask for more?
A life with laughter is never bland,
Take a seat and lend a hand.

Whimsical Whispers

A snail with a cape slides down a hill,
Winked at by ants, they gasp in thrill.
He takes on the world with a charming grin,
As the breeze carries giggles, where to begin?

In the café of clouds, jokes are brewed,
With coffee that tickles and laughter pursued.
Sugar spills over in sweet delight,
As whispers of whimsy take to flight.

Frogs in bow ties leap on and off,
While ducks throw in their hilarious scoff.
Each splash a punctuation of pure delight,
In the theater of joy, there's never a fight.

So, dance in the puddles of mirth and play,
Let giggles be guides on this wacky way.
With quirky tales and bold imagination,
We'll spin a world of joy, no hesitation.

Chronicles of Cheer

Once there was a cat dressed in pink,
With a top hat atop, what do you think?
She parades around town with struts so fine,
While the townsfolk giggle and sip their wine.

A bear on a skateboard whizzes by fast,
Causing a ruckus, but what a blast!
With each flip and tumble, joy echoing wide,
The forest is buzzing, laughter our guide.

In the market, a clown spills all the beans,
Mixing up veggies with sweet tangerines.
Each squishy sound brings a chorus of glee,
As folks pause to join in the merriment spree.

Together we gather, a jubilant tribe,
From pranks to jokes, oh, how we vibe!
Each story shared, an encyclopedia of fun,
As shadows grow long, the day is not done.

Giggles in the Glen

In a glen where the fringes of laughter meet,
A squirrel in a tutu spins on its feet.
While daisies gossip about the best snack,
The sun beams down, giving warmth to the pack.

A frog takes a leap but trips on a stone,
And lands in a puddle, it gurgles a groan.
Yet waves of laughter rise up like the tide,
As friends rush to help with giggles so wide.

The wind carries whispers of silly delight,
As butterflies dance, colors vibrant and bright.
In the backdrop of cackles and mischievous plans,
The world feels light, and joy always spans.

So come join the fun as we spin and we twirl,
In this glen of hilarity, laughter's our pearl.
With hearts full of humor, we'll make our own cheer,
Every giggle a treasure, bringing us near.

Mirthful Mornings in the Thicket

In the thicket, birds sing loud,
Squirrels dance, they're feeling proud.
A raccoon wears a silly hat,
As laughter echoes, short and fat.

Sunlight tickles leafy greens,
While rabbits share their silly scenes.
A turtle slips, a stumble here,
Froggy leaps, the crowd gives cheer.

Bumblebees buzz a happy tune,
Chasing shadows, feeling swoon.
With every giggle, joy takes flight,
Morning's warmth, a pure delight.

When nature plays its lighthearted game,
We'll never find the world the same.
For laughter blooms beneath the trees,
Inviting smiles with every breeze.

Laughter's Serenade Among the Branches

Amid the branches, shadows sway,
Squirrels chat the hours away.
A chipmunk shares a pie recipe,
While crickets play a melody.

Underneath a laughing sky,
A clumsy deer trips by, oh my!
With twirls and spins, the meadow plays,
As mischief brews in childish ways.

The trees wear coats of vibrant hues,
While chubby bunnies share their views.
A parrot cracks a joke or two,
Cheeks puffed up, a colorful view.

Nature's stage, where joy will reign,
In every laugh, there's no more pain.
In every rustle, every cheer,
The heart will know that fun is near.

Frolicsome Fables of the Woodlands

In woodlands deep, where stories weave,
A fox spins tales, we can't believe.
With twinkling eyes and floppy ears,
He shares his secrets, prompts our cheers.

The owls hoot, so wise and bold,
While tiny mice share laughter's gold.
A cackle here, a giggle there,
Echoes dance upon the air.

With every step, the forest jests,
A timid deer, in skirts, with zest.
A raccoon, nimble, steals the show,
As laughter spreads, it's time to grow.

Under the boughs, we come alive,
In joyous tales, we laugh and thrive.
As nature spins its frolicsome fables,
In every heart, the joy enshrouds like cables.

Joyful Resonance of the Green

In grassy fields where giggles bloom,
A gentle breeze scatters the gloom.
With every chuckle, shadows play,
As sunbeams dance throughout the day.

A playful hare makes funny faces,
While butterflies flit to joyous places.
The world grows lighter in this state,
Where every moment feels just great.

Each flower sways to laughter's sound,
As nature's joy spins round and round.
In every giggle, hope aligns,
With loving warmth, the heart entwines.

So gather round in this lovely scene,
Embrace the laughter, soft and keen.
In the vibrant realm of green we find,
A joyful resonance that twines the mind.

The Saga of Silliness

In a town where giggles bloom,
Cats wear hats, dispelling gloom.
Silly dances fill the square,
Umbrellas twirl in the warm spring air.

Jokes are told with playful flair,
Witty quips float everywhere.
Even grumpy gnomes join in,
With snickers hiding beneath their chin.

Bubbles rise like blushing cheeks,
Laughter echoes, laughter peaks.
A rubber chicken's on the run,
Chasing joy, oh what fun!

So gather 'round, let spirits soar,
In this world, there's always more.
The saga thrives, as the fun grows,
Embrace the chaos, let humor flow.

The Festival of Fun

Balloons burst with colors bright,
Clown shoes squeak, what a sight!
The pie-throwing contest, oh dear!
Faces smeared from ear to ear.

Silly hats atop each head,
As laughter dances, joy is spread.
Songs of goofiness fill the air,
People twirling without a care.

Juggling jellybeans, what a treat!
Kittens prancing on tiny feet.
Games are played right till the end,
With friends surrounding, laughter's blend.

A silly tale, a prank or two,
In this festival, smiles break through.
Whimsical joys we hold so dear,
In our hearts, the fun is clear.

Smiles Sown

In every nook, a chuckle grows,
Where every garden softly glows.
The seeds of joy are gently sown,
Tending laughter we've always known.

Puppies play in playful chases,
While silly selfies fill the spaces.
Each giggle blooms like springtime flowers,
Bringing bliss in giddy hours.

Knock-knock jokes on every door,
Unexpected, never a bore!
Weaving tales of fun and cheer,
Finding humor may bring a tear.

So plant your smiles, watch them rise,
Like the sun in playful skies.
No greater gift can one have shown,
Than laughter shared, and love grown.

Kaleidoscope of Kicks

Colors swirl in laughter's dance,
Every moment, a wacky chance.
Step right up, don't be shy,
Jump in the fun, let spirits fly!

In this realm where giggles reign,
Jokes are spun like a carnival train.
Tickling ribs, like softest tease,
Sparkling smiles, a joyous breeze.

Twists and turns, a bright parade,
Silly antics never fade.
Swinging high on swings of glee,
Find yourself in silly jubilee.

A mosaic of whims, bright delight,
With every kick, we take to flight.
In laughter's arms, we spin and sway,
A world of whimsy, come what may.

Harbingers of Happiness

A jester slips on a banana peel,
The crowd bursts into a hearty squeal.
With every trip and silly dance,
Laughter blooms at every chance.

Tickled by tales of clumsy grace,
Smiles spread wide on every face.
A joke tossed like a playful ball,
We gather round, we laugh, we fall.

Giggling echoes through the air,
A chorus of joy, beyond compare.
In these moments, worries flee,
The world is light as we all agree.

Who knew that laughter was the key,
To unlock joy, so wild and free?
In every chuckle, we find our song,
Together in laughter, we all belong.

Mirage of Mirth

In a world where tickles reign,
Giggles sprout like summer rain.
A mirage forms of smiles and jokes,
Brightening the hearts of all who stoke.

Pranks abound with a wink and grin,
Chasing frowns away, let joy begin.
A playful banter, like a river, flows,
In the desert of gloom, laughter grows.

Witty remarks that flutter and fly,
Turn our sighs into gleeful high.
Around the campfire, stories unfold,
Each tale wrapped in warmth, a joy to behold.

We dance in delight, no care in sight,
In the mirage of joy, everything feels right.
With every chuckle like a spark igniting,
Mirth is the magic, endlessly inviting.

Threads of Thrills

Through the fabric of joy, we weave,
Threads of laughter that never leave.
Each stitch a moment, knitted tight,
Crafted from giggles that burst with light.

A silly hat or a bouncing shoe,
These vibrant strands make life anew.
With every twist and every turn,
Laughter flickers, a flame we yearn.

We toss around our witty lines,
In the tapestry of life, laughter shines.
A patchwork quilt of humor bright,
Warming the heart, a pure delight.

In the loom of time, our spirits lift,
As we share this joyous gift.
We gather close, united still,
In threads of thrill, we find our fill.

Euphoria in the Ether

A funny face, a goofy glide,
Creates a bubble where we confide.
In ether bright, joy takes its flight,
Tickling souls from morning to night.

Whispers of chuckles float in the air,
Invisible waves that lift our care.
A sparkle, a wink, a knowing glance,
Summon the magic, invite the dance.

Jests that soar like kites on strings,
We grasp the joy that laughter brings.
In every burst, in every cheer,
Euphoria wraps us, drawing near.

So let us raise a toast of glee,
To bubbling laughter, wild and free.
In this ether where we play,
Euphoria reigns, come what may.

Laughter in the Leafy Hideaway

In the shade where whispers play,
Squirrels dance without delay.
A chirping bird joins in the chase,
Tickling smiles on every face.

The breeze carries a silly sound,
As giggles echo all around.
Frolicsome frogs leap with glee,
Turning every frown to spree.

Under branches thick and green,
You'll find the silliest scene.
Nature's jokes take flight and soar,
While critters jump and laugh for more.

So come and join this merry spree,
Where laughter flows like a wild sea.
In this hideaway of cheer,
Every worry disappears!

Rhapsody of the Giggle Grove

In the grove where shadows play,
Joyful echoes come what may.
A tumbleweed rolls with flair,
While rabbits giggle in the air.

Breezes hum a comic tune,
Dancing fireflies light the moon.
With every leap and bound they share,
The trees snicker, unaware.

A symphony of chuckles rise,
With sunlit sparks that mesmerize.
Laughter weaves through every crease,
In this place where joy won't cease.

So grab a friend, come take your chance,
Join the woodland's jolly dance.
In this grove, fun has its reign,
Forever laughs shall entertain!

The Woodland Revelers' Anthem

In the heart of darkened woods,
Jesters frolic in the hoods.
A mischievous breeze whispers fear,
But all it brings is hearty cheer.

Mushrooms sprout with faces bright,
As laughter echoes through the night.
Every nook and cranny hums,
With silly tales and playful drums.

The owls hoot a giggling tune,
While raccoons dance beneath the moon.
Branches sway as critters glide,
In this merry, wild ride.

So gather 'round, both far and near,
Embrace the joy that brings us here.
With every chuckle, every smile,
The woodland revelers beguile!

Joy in the Heart of Nature's Stage

Underneath the towering pines,
Where laughter flows like joyful lines.
Nature's stage, a playful breeze,
Sets the scene with utmost ease.

A plump raccoon wears a hat,
Dancing wild, oh look at that!
With every twirl, a giggle lands,
As woodland creatures join in bands.

The flowers sway, their petals bright,
Tickled pink by sheer delight.
With butterflies that float and spin,
In this show, let joy begin!

So come and take your seat and laugh,
At this merry nature's half.
In every laugh, in every cheer,
The heart of nature draws you near!

The Tome of Tittering

In a world of giggles, tales unfold,
A jester's quip, worth its weight in gold.
Bouncing puns on a trampoline,
Shared in whispers, oh so serene.

Laughter dances on the breeze,
Tickles shadows, sways the trees.
A feathered hat atop a cat,
Jumps and jests, imagine that!

In each nook, a chuckle hides,
With silly socks and joyous rides.
Guffaws ringing, hearts in flight,
Chasing giggles into the night.

Turn the page, let fever pitch,
Mirth ignites, a grand old switch.
In this tome where joy abounds,
Each line a laughter, life resounds.

Radiant Ripples

A puddle splashes, laughter leaps,
Sunlit smiles, a secret keeps.
Frogs in bow ties sing their song,
Skip around, where fun belongs.

Jokes on waves, the sea responds,
Bubbles burst, and joy absconds.
Tickled toes in sandy shores,
Every wave brings laughs galore.

Silly hats on sea turtles race,
Splashing joy, a funny chase.
Mermaids giggle, tails entwined,
Rippling echoes, sweetly aligned.

In the whirl of water's play,
Laughter brightens up the day.
Radiant ripples all around,
Joy in motion, laughter found.

Laughter's Legacy

Across the ages, echoes cheer,
Tales of folly, crystal clear.
A dad joke slips, a child grins,
In each heart, the chuckle spins.

Foolish kings in courtly jest,
Wear their crowns with humor pressed.
Silly stories told at night,
Whimsical dreams in laughter's light.

A whoopee cushion's classic prank,
Brings smiles forth, a hearty rank.
With every giggle, bonds are made,
In humor's glow, love won't fade.

So cherish laughs, the legacy,
Passed through time, eternity.
In joy we find our truest thread,
With laughter's gift, we forge ahead.

Festive Fables

In jolly streets, the stories rise,
Silly sprinkles, playful pies.
Elves with tricks and dancing fire,
Mirthful tales we all admire.

Gnomes that giggle, fairies that tease,
Tales unfold like autumn leaves.
A talking dog with quite a tale,
Whispers laughter on the gale.

Bright balloons and playful glee,
Magic moments wild and free.
Each fable spun, a merry twist,
In merry hearts, there's not a mist.

So gather round, let laughter soar,
In every word, adventure's core.
Festive fables, joys we make,
Shimmering memories, never break.

www.ingramcontent.com/pod-product-compliance
Lightning Source LLC
Chambersburg PA
CBHW051656160426
43209CB00004B/920